Recognizing the Stranger in the Mirror

It's You!

Stacey Bulluck

Contents

Introduction

The ice dam I was engulfed in hardened my heart, freezing all dreams. Perhaps most importantly, the free and private space needed for my growing mind to play, explore, reflect, and exercise creative imaginations was deemed unworthy. This powerful resource and valuable link to my dreams were frozen by the need to survive. I needed to live.

September 1990 in Fairbanks, Alaska, my outlook of the journey began to shift, and my heart started healing. Although the following 22 years had some turbulent moments, I am here today as evidence of the God substance we are made in the image of. Now 30 years later has passed, and I am making my contribution to the earth through the gift of writing. Right before this book, I was blessed to write a chapter in a book called *I Am My Sister's Keeper*, with 16 other women, and we became bestselling authors on Amazon. My chapter is called "Healing of My Heart," which is a process that started a long time ago. Aligning with my sisters of kindred experiences. All having healing stories to share. Revealing snippets of our journeys. As my heart was being healed, all the pain, disappointment, fear, brokenness, etc. were transformed to massive amounts of love. Enough love to fill all the foundational cracks that were left unattended. See, my foundation was scarred upon arrival, and the marring continued well into my mid-forties. I do not blame any of the attempts to damage my mortal being or the attempt to obliterate my soul's purpose on anyone or anything. Here I stand at this mirror allowing the light of love to shine in, igniting the wicks of my purpose to come to life. Allowing the warmth of the glow from within to be the salve needed to inflame and dissolve a cold and brutal outlook on life. Selah.

WHO I BE

Someone, please come tell me who I be.

Who I be?

Am I the scared little girl afraid of the bullies across the street who turned out not to be a match for the fight in me or am I the isolated family member looked upon as an outcast because I'm the only child, and there must be something wrong with me? Somehow, eye sights closest to me saw this outward image, this persona that "you must think you're better than everybody else." Who me, but if you could only see on the inside the girl who couldn't see past the tears cried and no one hears. Who I be, the little girl who doesn't even remember going from house-to-house and how it all happened the abandoned child, the 13-year-old exposed to sexual activity by someone who had no business destroying the innocence of her childhood?

Who I be?

The four-year-old who took a ride halfway across the country thinking she was going on a family trip when it turned out she was going to be dropped off again, dropped off to the hands of sin, dropped off to a plate filled with Raid, dropped off to a fit of rage? Anger that attempted suffocation. Once angry confused little girl still tried to see who I be.

Am I the label of PTSD because humanity disregarded my safety? Am I the angry black woman I was often described as?

Hell no, I fit in not one of those categories. Some 50+ years, later this chocolate girl stands before you as a bold, beautiful, black Queen. Flowing in her streams, manifesting her dreams, filling the canvas of life with her BEING. BEING!

Her existence brings light; her light gives life. Who I Be Huldah the prophetess being the gatekeeper of her city? Who I be Ruth who demonstrates unwavering faith or Deborah a woman of integrity who is a leader among leaders?

This chocolate Queen right here knows who I be. I am beautifully and wonderfully made in the image of a power so strong it will turn your dark clouds into light, directing your path as the magnificent glow of who I BE. I shine, giving vitality, bringing peace and most of all showers of love. So, who I be a life-giving source of energy spreading love and sharing hope? BEING and becoming; becoming and being.

The more I'm connected to this frequency the more I understand that nobody can come and tell me who I BE I must discover from within that I am this strong beautiful Queen.

We Must Ask Ourselves Hard Questions

In my last book, *Don't Let Your Brain Go Numb: Regaining Power Through Resilience,* I state in chapter 1, "Without Feeling or Sensation," "you do not have the ability to realize." Meaning, when the mind is without understanding, it will not send messages to the body. Here is when we are stripped of the power to comprehend, stripped of the power to realize, and stripped of the power to appropriately respond. In that case it was a person not having awareness that they are stuck. Not having the ability to realize that life has come to a stop. This individual is no longer engaging in the process of life. The desire to move forward or past a point; it could be a point of pain, despair, rejection, insecurity, we could go on and on, but I believe you get it. The desire is gone. Where did it go? Who has it? Why did it leave? Most importantly, how do we get it back? That is the question of the day!

Because we are asking questions, this is a clear indication that something has compelled us to want to move past this point in our lives. Yes, it is most likely the same point which caused us to bury the desire in the first place. Often the things that cause us to stop are the same things that cause us to grow. It could be just as simple as we have come to the end of a thing, but we continue to hold to the something that is finished. It has played its role and is no longer viable, no longer capable of working successfully. In other words, it no longer serves us.

But today is the day of desired resurrection! Somehow, we allowed the point of the wrong belief to become the focus. Now what we allowed to become the center of attention is sending signals to our mind saying that we chose to accept rejection and insecurity as our truth, BUT (Believers Understanding Truth) know that is the biggest lie ever told.

The lie can cause your creative instinct to die. This dark mindset breeds an emptiness where **wanting, desiring, and craving to** BE who you truly are becomes past tense in your mind. Then our ability to hope for a thing, is far in the recesses of our mind. Do not go to the place of nothingness where you have placed you on the back burner. It is time to take a stand and recognize who you are.

Where, When, and How Did This Happen?

I had to do my due diligence and make sure that we have clarity on where we are cognitively when we become emotionally wounded. Notice I did not say when we experience psychological pain. Having an experience is inevitable. Because we are alive and live around other humans. Because desire is a verb that means action is required and we cannot allow a temporary short-lived period to cause us to be dwindled down far in a place that seems hopeless and far beyond return to keep us paralyzed. So far gone you are swimming in the demonstrative sea of despair. Hanging out in thoughts that become overwhelming where the course will lead, and then we begin to believe this is how life should be. When thoughts of despair in the mind are left to roam free in our mind this could dictate how we function or NOT function in life. I heard something the other day, while listening to some motivational speeches. The gentleman said and I am paraphrasing, what are heading toward failure or prosperity? This said to me there are ways to go, and it is my choice which direction I go in. The same is true for you. Because you are engaged here right now, reading this book I believe for the purpose of bringing back to life your visions, passions and aspirations which seem to have receded into an ibis of darkness. That you have made a choice to aim toward prosperity. Not just tangible gain, but more importantly an invisible gain inwardly. This is where the strength of who you are lives.

Back to recess or the temporary short-term moment discussed earlier. Let me share how it intrigued me. Recesses according to Microsoft Smart Lookup means to be suspended. You know like being suspended from school it's not permanent. The individual just does not show up for a few days, but it is temporary. So, since this is simply a short-term interruption to the act of aspiring or having a yearning for something; there must be a process that will interrupt the transitory interruption and cause the flow of life and vitality and get us back on track. Oh, remember the student will eventually be allowed to go back to school. Now! We are on to something, and the next step is to act! It is time to go back to the school of BEING, dreaming, expecting, and the best place to be in is in love with you.

Let's stop here and promise to never stop becoming your authentic self. Always love you. Once we pick up speed never allow yourself to bring your momentum to a screeching halt. Yes, we might have to slow down and rest, but stopping is not an option. In other words, giving up is no longer in your being. No longer in your DNA (Devine Nature Activated).

Keep reading and through the crevices of these pages I hope you are driven and filled with a passion for your purpose. Come on, delve into the lessons with me!

It Is Time to Come to Oneself, to a Better Mind

While going along on this journey, it is a great awareness to know who you are. Allow yourself to receive the grace needed for the next leg of the journey. It may take time to build healthy habits, which eventually become a lifestyle that will push you through all the oppositions that will come your way. I know we are just in the first chapter and for some this is literally the first chapter of your brand-new life. We have made some decisions to get us to this point. Some great, some good, maybe some mediocre, and then there are those decisions which we need to see them come to their final resting place. This will take some doing on our part, but (Believers Understanding Truth) know the time is now.

Say this, I am open to all the great possibilities I was born for. I am limitless, I am getting out of my own way. My thoughts of who I am are great and not of a lesser value. My mind produces thoughts of excellence. My body follows excellence. Everything I touch turns to gold. This is the perception received in our senses when we allow our mind to trust in the divine plan already established for you and me.

There is a story that tells of a son who was given the opportunity to realize that greatness was instilled in him right in the middle of his horrible experience, which by the way, was his choice. Somewhere during his time of literally spending days and nights lying in pig slop he came to his senses. He came to a better mind. Before his dreadful decision he was living in the house with a father who apparently was a wise man. He was wise enough to have an inheritance for his children that this son figured he would ask for before it was time for him to have it. I sincerely hope you grasp the meaning of the last sentence. Now, back to the story. The father, through forming good habits demonstrated this good stewardship and now the son is coming back to the abilities he had developed prior to his poor decision. The wisdom and strength of the father that was taught gave him the ability to push through his foolish ways and ideas, which produced this event to begin with. However, I am not here to discount his experience because it brought him to a place of knowing who he was. I love these small but powerful phrases: "But when he [finally] came to his senses, he said, I will get up and go…" (Luke15:17-18).

Coming to oneself could possibly bring rawness, meaning there is a full gamut of emotions flowing through our cognitive system at the same time. Scrubbing away all the unnecessary elements clogging our view of us. In my case it feels as if my heart, the depths of all that is within me, is on full display. There is nowhere to hide, there is no concealer. Every passionate, private, and personal place that is vibrating within has made its way to the surface and it is right in my face. Beckoning with an unyielding, unwavering tug on my soul. The reality of who you are is staring you in the face and its time we recognize this BEing. This being is YOU strong and confident in who you are. Even with all the mistakes and flaws the moment of recognition is front and center and you are more ready than you know to use your pot of clay, your human frame for its planned purposes. A plan that was put into motion before our arrival. I have been enlightened a little further about the "get off the pot or pee" syndrome. This says if you are not going to believe in who you are then get off the pot, but if you are choosing to use the pot for its intended reason then do it. I know weird analogy, yet the essence is there. We have been intentionally designed and if we are not going to recognize who we are and use our gifts and talents that is catastrophic for the ones who we are connected to our gift because they are waiting for us to show up. It is time to come to our self, speak your truth, and move forward.

I believe you and I have come to the same moment of identification, and we want to show up. We are choosing to BE clearly visible in this world. We will not stop until the tugging stops, but I must warn you once you have begun using this pot of clay for its intended purpose the flow is ***eternal and there is no stopping***. Once you give the sign of the slightest bit of yes to your purpose you cannot stop the building process if you tried.

Isaiah 64:8

You, LORD, are our Father. We are nothing but clay, but you are the potter who molded us.

Ecclesiastes 3:11 Amplified Bible (AMP) God Set Eternity in the Heart of Man

11 He has made everything beautiful and appropriate in its time. He has also planted eternity [a sense of divine purpose] in the human heart [a mysterious longing which nothing under the sun can satisfy, except God]—yet man cannot find out (comprehend,

grasp) what God has done (His overall plan) from the beginning to the end.

We are wired to desire, crave, create, and develop. However, it can be hard to do when what we see in the mirror we do not recognize. The BEing side says hey let me show you something or should I say show you someone. Our mirror is internal. We have been trained to use the outer mirror but the mirror we need for understanding how to see all the way through, is the mirror of our mind. Our mind is the connection to our soul. You know the cliché "the eyes are the window to the soul." Yes, but the eyes are within. Just as the cliché says we are looking into the soul. The place where our thoughts, passions, and desires collide. The place where dreams are birthed, and progress is pushed. The intense pursuit produces a tangible evidence put on full display, giving us moments of enjoyment, with pleasure gushing for the world to see and experience. I believe we have come to this portion of the journey where we are no longer looking in the window wishing but are now in the position of producing. Putting action to our thoughts. Creating and delivering what we see within.

Perhaps you have not come to a place of understanding what you see, yet. Take this moment to ask out loud for clarity of directions for the next steps to fulfilling what you see. Keep in mind, these moments come in brief sections of time, and we are responsible for taking full advantage of them when they arrive. If for some reason in this flash of time, your inner view is not clear, I ask you to give you permission to see beyond. Look inside of the person you are believing yourself to be. Any mistakes, things you may see as flaws, such as education, economic, or income level, those things do not matter when it comes to the mirror of your soul. You must declare your own freedom. It is time to unveil your identity. There is an eternal desire in you waiting to make an appearance and never to be veiled again.

Loving Who I See

Appreciation of who you are is first on the agenda of loving you. It is a powerful thing to love and adore yourself. When we know this type of love and support in our inner man and have this awareness, there is nothing outside of you that can stop you from achieving all you aim to do.

This kind of admiration is of the deepest kind. It goes far beyond the surface. You know the superficial stuff, hair, clothes, physique, money, etc. Most humans equate the appreciation of themselves according to what they see on the outside. They welcome a nice body, beautiful hair, and stylish clothing. All of these things are seen by the human eye.

The esteem we need to display toward ourselves pushes us to put an end to any thoughts stored in our mind saying we have no value. It WILL cause us to believe in the value of who we are. This appreciation comes from within. There will be moments when our ability to produce self-esteem in mega doses must be our superpower. That keeps us from retreating to old behaviors once displayed when others try to disregard our worth. It is time to understand your worth and allow the gifts and treasures to be displayed on the earth's canvas. Let us go within and bring forward talents and abilities. Bring your offerings as spiritual beings. We must deposit our contributions of service in the earth. However, first we must raise our level of believing and become confident we deserve to be this great conduit of riches.

Recognizing Your Worth

To recognize means to "know exactly," to realize without having any discrepancy or deception about your worthiness. This insight will cause an escalation of thought regarding who you are. You will begin to accept the role as the channel which carries riches from place to place. Because you are spiritual, capable, intelligent, and virtuous.

Proverbs 31:10

An excellent woman [one who is spiritual, capable, intelligent, and virtuous], who is he who can find her? Her value is more precious than jewels and her worth is far above rubies or pearls.

Note: The pronoun depicted here as her is descriptive of the house of God, and if the world crisis has not taught us anything it should have taught us the place of Gods dwelling is not in brick and mortar. Just as He placed His physical seed in a woman. She became the dwelling place of God until His natural emergence. When will you allow your behavior to be that of someone who knows your worth is far above any earthly jewel created? You are the dwelling place of God.

James 1:17-18 The Message Translation

16-18 So, my very dear friends, don't get thrown off course. Every desirable and beneficial gift comes out of heaven. The gifts are rivers of light cascading down from the Father of Light. There is nothing deceitful in God, nothing two-faced, nothing fickle. He brought us to life using the true Word, showing us off as the crown of all his creatures.

God says your worthy to be a crown created just for His glory. I can imagine us shining through all the circumstances that come while we are going along the way. There is no time to allow discouragement to win. It is time to trust and believe we are capable of BEING the best representations of Gods crown which is formed in greatness and power to accomplish our life's intended purpose as a spiritual being who can formulate intelligent and good practices that lead to an enhanced life.

The meaning of being spiritual these days has taken on such a vast perspective, but I want to say, it is not something to be considered as spooky or religious. From my point of view, spirituality refers to someone who lives their daily life being guided by a force that is much greater than we are. As spiritual beings, the power within us provides all we need to live a life filled with Godly principles. An example of this would be when we choose to do right or wrong. We choose to follow what is morally right because right sets us up for good and wrong sets us up for failure. When I say right and wrong, this pertains to moments of quick judgement where the outcome may be good, but the action to get too good is wrong. Reads simple, right? I am chuckling here because when things seem simple, they often are produced through what we cannot see. Like through the thoughts entertained in our minds before the behavior is exposed. It is in that space of time we are given the opportunity of choice. Between the thought and the action of the thought. Here is where we acknowledge we have the power of choice. The choice is made according to our certainty of our value. When we are confident of our significance there is understanding. Knowledge it is simply not at our level, and we decide with wisdom leading the way. I could not think of a better way to help you understand your full value other than to share the verse below.

This snatched my heart strings and immediately provided the insight needed to fully sum up who we are and how significant we are on earth. Ambassadors of riches. Especially when we choose to BE the distributor of these riches. Surrendered to the marvelous spiritual being who is created in the likeness and image of greatness is on display for all to see.

Psalm 139:13-16 The Message Translation

"Oh yes, you shaped me first inside, then out; you formed me in my mother's womb. I thank you, High God—you're breathtaking! Body and soul, I am marvelously made! I worship in adoration—what a creation! You know me inside and out, you know every bone in my body; You know exactly how I was made, bit by bit, how I was sculpted from nothing into something. Like an open book, you watched me grow from conception to birth; all the stages of my life were spread out before you, The days of my life all prepared before I'd even lived one day."

Accept that you are great regardless of some of the behaviors you have exhibited in the past that may not have been so wonderful. They are not a determination of who we are spiritually, and it certainly does not determine the outcome of our lives. There is a reason why our physical growth was carefully monitored during our developmental process in the womb. From the time of conception to our emergence God saw you, you were in full view, and there is an expectation of who was be sculpted, some say knitting together. Joint by joint, piece by piece you are the work of art that is cherished and loved.

Now our eyes are opened and vision becoming clearer every day. This will only turn out well when we are committed to continuing the process of recognition and appreciation for who we are. No more downplaying our own greatness. No more allowing our ideas to self-destruct in our own minds before they have an opportunity to develop and be displayed for all to see. We are worth it! Say it out loud I AM WORTH IT!

Being Honest with Myself

Did you know that every sixty-eight seconds someone downplays our gifts and talents and lead us to a spiral of self-doubt, which could pave the road for procrastination. Yes, I said the dirty word. At least, in my life this word was tabu. Because for a long time I did not tell myself the truth. There is a passage that says, "the truth will make you free." My interpretation of this is, when truth is allowed to lead the way all the necessary ingredients needed to get us to a point of being unrestricted and giving permission for the real BEING to spring from the infinite well of possibilities shows up. No limits on how much of you, you can be. Take the constraints off, you have the power to remove your own handcuffs. Handcuffs of hesitation, uncertainty, and reservations. The only time we need reservations is for dinner. Go ahead I know you laughed. Seriously though, stop the lies of telling yourself my flaws and what I like to call (idio-secret-sees) idiosyncrasies, our peculiar ways are imperfections controlling how far you will go in life. Let us become free in our overstanding. Come on say it out loud, today I remove any thought in my conscious and subconscious mind that gives me mis and disinformation. Anything that comes with the intent of deception about who I AM no longer has a position here. We are seeing and acting with our awareness and keen senses. Without restrictions of space, capacity, or the amount of power we possess. From this moment on, it is your responsibility to always eliminate any slanted perceptions of who you are. Tell yourself the truth. Halt thoughts that give life to outside entities. Silence the thoughts produced by external temporary satisfaction. Practice building on the good and greatness in you will show up well developed.

Abandoned Thoughts

Brick walls were erected early in my life when I was in The thought of dreaming had escaped my being for a long time. My experiences and traumas had stolen my ability to dream and delight in joy and pleasure. Honestly, I was sure every day came adorned with doom and gloom. Therefore, my actions were accommodating to the thoughts of someone who felt unworthy, helpless, and numb. Clearly showing how the act of abandoning thoughts and visualization of life outside of what was I taught or not taught, had left its imprint in my mind. Be careful what you allow in your view on a consistent basis. According to Medford Medical Care, "your eyesight is one of your most important senses: 80% of what we perceive comes through our sense of sight." Your sense of sight is your power to perceive. Your power to have vision.

In the early '80s the average middle-class family perceived it was a great accomplishment if your child went to college and that was especially true if you were a black child being raised in a single parent home like me. Families have this as an aspiration for their offspring. This was a thriving time for Black people politically, Jesse Jackson had a national campaign running for President of the United States, but it also was just twenty years prior that Black people were marching for voting rights and pure human equality. There were separate drinking fountains, labeling who should use what in public settings. But, during that time signs of opportunity to envision life different were in sight. However, things that come into our sight path are not always what they appear to be. Blacks were on the rise and being recognized.

Note: Stopping and pondering on that statement was something I did when I heard it in my mind, but more impacting is what I felt in my heart.

Still even in times where a collective is appearing to advance, we cannot be swayed by what is seen. Stay true to who you see within. Let's not get mesmerized at the mere optical assisted view of something. This perception that life would be better for you when you see it and do it the way others do may be very far from your truth. Meaning that because society considered it socially and economically sound to become what others viewed as a respectable job everyone must go about attaining success in the same way. There is no guarantee if you do it their way you will have the same success. It is sad society equates success of human BEINGs according to another individual. Did you catch that? We are individuals, existing as our distinct self. I cannot be you and you cannot be me. We all have our originality or at least you should strive to be your distinct, unique, unapologetic self. Never place any weight or substance in a category of status. Because this status is simply reflective of what someone else feels is appropriate. It may not be appropriate for you. I remember when my daughter went to college, and I was so excited she was going to become a doctor and she received a full academic scholarship to do so. Then guess what she stopped going to college to become what my skewed vision had dreamed and aspired for. My then tainted experiences had interfered with her passion and vision. To allow the authenticity of who she is to come through. That is a dream killer of the worst kind because I made her feel like my dream was more important and the only way for her to become worthy is to follow the blueprint dictated by another's perception.

As parents we want the best for our children. But it is not our duty to tell them who they should because that was determined before they are in the womb of the mother. It is our duty to inspire them to dream and become that which gives them drive and fulfillment in their heart. We must remind them and those who are in our village never forget to dream. Guiding them in always knowing that you are worthy and capable of aspiration, having ambition, and producing ideas. These actions will cause you to consistently put forth effort to become. Changing, developing, becoming takes courage. In my case it would have been courage to say I did not want to be the things that were prominent in the eyes of others. Unfortunately, I did not know then what I needed, but now that I know it is necessary as I produce ideas to write, I must compose words in sentences with integrity. With the hope it compels others to have the courage needed to excel at developing the stranger we often see in the mirror.

This person is a stranger because our ears are receiving a message of those who thought the advice or commands, they were giving us were for our good, but the heart piece that was missing. You see, the issues of life, the being side of our humanity flows from this place of intimacy. Intimacy produces knowing who we are. Whomever they were that expressed their thoughts of who we are came from within them and were formed by their experiences. It is impossible for us to become them and vice versa they cannot become us.

We can never take on the persona of another human. Why? Because we have our own and it is a perfect fit. It is not our job to be who they imagine us to be. Seeing ourselves through another person's mind is worse than having a physical blindness. You are forced to move from house to house and this makes it extremely difficult to get your footing and calculation of steps from one piece of furniture to another. Now you continually stumble around bumping into things possibly hurting yourself at the same time. WOW!

Now that was a mouth full. You may want to take a minute to digest that. If I am sight challenged and I do not receive the proper training on how to navigate through life without physical eyesight most likely my view of life will also become a place I am blind to. I used to work for the National Federation of the Blind (NFB), in their headquarters office. They have thousands of gadgets and additional training aids to assist with the navigation process to enhance the quality of life for those challenged in their sense of sight. Now think of someone who's view/vision of who they are is not able to be seen because society, economics, culture, environment and or trauma etcetera, caused your heart to become unwilling to discern things to explore, dream of, or contemplate. This can be a reason why you abandon any thoughts or dreams and allow the courage you need to dissipate like a vapor into the air. Imagine the breath of life (pneuma), which is the creative force within you, no longer guides or prompts any innovation in your soul. When this happens your life canvas is painted by outside influences; the source within is covered in darkness and we become blinded to our own power. Without mindsight of who we are we develop into a distorted view, and we stumble and fall sometimes without the ability to get back up to the true view of who we are and the person we see in the mirror daily is a stranger.

Read on…

Remember earlier I said I used to work for the NFB, which was one of my stumbles I had when the pressures of life knocked me down, but thankfully I landed there. Although, I had not removed the blinders at this point they were slowly coming off. This was 2006 – 2007, two of my most challenging years. There was more to come and boy oh boy they were doozies. Not only did I work there, but this was one of my jobs on the way to getting here and writing. Forgive me I digress. Insert smile here. 😊

Back to the NFB. Working there gave me insight on how physically someone could navigate through life without eyesight. Many were attorney's, bookkeepers, political advocates, visionaries, but most of all enthusiastic about moving a specific population of humanity forward. I remember them having their annual meeting and people with white canes and red tips, the red tips are a signature of the NFB. Challenge sighted people would come from all over the country to get recharged for the upcoming year and the challenges they may face. However, they never spoke of those challenges as obstacles, and they would not allow those challenges to defeat them. The same goes for spiritual blindness, I say spiritual because we are spiritual beings having an experience in the realm of earth. It is time to remove the heart blinders and dream. Yes, dream again and if you are like me and do not have any memories of dreaming about BEING start today. I pray an igniting of excitement comes with all the necessity's you need to restore your heart to the place where creativity flows and the abundance of authenticity of who you are comes bursting through every day!

Abandoned Thoughts

Dreams deferred. Sent to a place of no longer existing. A place dry and desolate nothing flows there. Streams of dirt, rocks, and sand. Seemingly not a part of a plan or thought. No expression or demonstration of life. Purpose to fulfill no more just desolate, isolate, and barren. There is no life in you. That was the anthem daily sang. No reason

to be alive. Soul deprived. Just a flicker of light in a garden of despair. No drum beating to the rhythm of life. Hope deferred and my heart is sick, but I long for a life fulfilled. My longing produces a tree of life. A wellspring of understanding giving me expectancy, flowing brooks of wisdom guiding my heart navigation of my soul. Remove the blinders off my will, determination, and intellect. Free my soul. I long to be the creation I am. Wonderfully and fearfully made. All the necessary ingredients added. Strength of diamonds. Royalty of rubies. The dignity of peridot. I am a gem of the son. Walking in the brilliant light of courage. Inspired and confidently trusting my ability to move, live and have my being. I know I have what it takes to make it happen. Assured in an intimacy of a purpose I must fulfill. I owe the earth my imprint is needed here. Through your breath of life. I am alive again. Be spontaneous and free moving through eternity. My soul thirst for the manifestation of the created me. The me before the foundation of the world the me sculptured and formed. The real, the timeless me unlocked, unafraid, unchained me. The unabandoned me.

Allow Creativity to Flow

Flow through the tears and sometime years of spiritual blindness, which is the state of poor or no perception. It is the inability to see in your heart, cause your mind to perceive thoughts that produce understanding to develop and manifest who you are. Just as the words on these pages are flowing through my fingers on to this computer screen soon to be a tangible book for you to read and physically see is a demonstration of having the ability to discern what is in my heart. Pulling out what my inner man sees, transport it through my mind and show it to the world in a book. As spirit beings belonging to the source of Spirit, we are responsible for building what we are to share with the world. Not everyone is going to share literary art, like this book, not everyone is going to share the art of cosmetology or fabulous culinary skills or create ways for others to lose weight, tone our bodies and so on.

Therefore, it is imperative we take responsibility for filling the earth with our gifts. I say it this way, simply doing your part.

Pour some paint remover of love on your canvas covered in another's idea of who you are. Start with loving you unconditionally, without judgement of the past regardless of how you see physically it. Take off the cloudy scratched up lens. Take the lens out, in fact take the broken, skewed, glasses off. The prescription is wrong.

I remember a few years ago having the wrong eyeglass prescription. When I left the optometry office and as I walked to my vehicle, I noticed the view through the new lens was off. Way off to the point where I felt ill. I was off balance. My body felt as if I could not get my proper footing. It was as if the ground were not reachable. This was a horrible feeling.

For those of us who wear glasses, it has been said that if we are not able to see properly after wearing new glasses for a couple of weeks and it does not improve the "prescription may be too weak or too strong." This happens sometimes, and it can cause headaches, eye strain, and fatigue. However, for adults, it is nothing to worry about in the long term. Getting the correct prescription means that you suffer less eye strain. When we decide to get the right prescription, we do not have to strain to see. Think about it like this, it is no longer a strain to receive instructions about who we are. Straining is what causes damage it is not our lack of ability to see. Depending on how we see will determine the level of struggling to comprehend who we are therefore it will be difficult manifesting who we are.

Once we get those things out of the way that we have strained so hard for and really they did not serve us anymore. Because of the constant force, we have caused our own damage. Often our pressures become a distraction and gives access to the possibility of experiencing the loss of focus. Then for some strange reason we oppose wearing glasses (we are focusing on the glasses instead of the asset they are to our sight) because our visual acuity is skewed. With skewed spiritual vision it is near impossible to believe the truth of who you are and who you can strive to become. Remember, that the place where the vision comes from is still in there untouched just waiting for us to stop paying attention to the small disturbances that came in the form illustrated by the headache and eye strain we get from stressing. In other words, giving ourselves unnecessary tension. The best thing we can do to alleviate the pressure is accept the truth and get to the real matter. Move forward and get the right prescription for our eyes. Do not just give up on the glasses, which is a tool to assist us with sight.

Let us equate this to having the right prescription for achieving life goals. Having the right instructions and direction for our lives gives us that 20/20 vision. According to American Optometric Association, "20/20 vision is normal vision acuity (the clarity or sharpness of vision) from the distance of 20 feet." If you have 20/20 vision, you can see clearly and are able to make out letters from 20 feet away. The goal is to have a precise vision to see out in the distance. We want to have vision without strain to see past the voids of life. The empty spaces we may feel is far too much for us to fill. Believe you can fulfill purpose. Right now, you are doing the work. You are reading this book and the details of these words are infusing any area of you that feels empty. When our life vision is viewed through clear thinking, keen awareness, coherent and with pure intent. Our new life anthem is I can see clearly now that the strain is gone. There is no more fight in knowing, accepting, trusting, and believing who we are. The essence of my complete entire BEING will no longer accept the wrong prescription, the wrong instructions. Say it, I am clear about who I am; I am astute about who I am; I have sound thoughts about who I am: I am genuine in heart.

Everything we need is already within us. As we learn more about who we are, we grow and are eager do our utmost to present ourselves to God approved (tested by trial). Ready to work having no cause to be ashamed, guilty, or unequipped.

2 Peter 1:3 Contemporary English Version

3 We have everything we need to live a life that pleases God. It was all given to us by God's own power, when we learned he had invited us to share in his wonderful goodness.

Always remain teachable because there is for certain a test called life and you must be ready when it comes. This test comes to prove to you and I and those who are watching. They are waiting for the greatness in us to appear. It is up to you and me to know what we are to show up as.

After serving in the Army for the first six-years of my eighteen-year career, it was time to accept the next test. I submitted a request to go from being a dental assistant to becoming a dental hygienist and the Army accepted my application. While taking this course, oh and let me add in here I was two-months pregnant and about to spend the next sixteen weeks away from what I considered home at that time. This included my daughter who was seven-years old. She went to stay with my mom, another new test and of course, when I applied, I was not pregnant. Okay, back to where I was, we knew every week it was a requirement to take a quiz and a test. This course was rigorous! The military condensed a two-year college level course into sixteen weeks. It was sometime brutal.

Once a week, our minds would face a test and if we had not prepared ourselves for it, let me say that again, if we had not prepared ourselves, most likely we would fail. We could prepare to pass, or we could prepare to fail. No one came each day and asked us if we studied. It was the student's responsibility to make sure we were ready for use, making sure when we returned to the dental clinic, at our duty station we were ready to contribute to the productivity of the office. We gained this skill through obtaining the necessary knowledge to pass every week. I smiled here because I thought of the days and nights we studied until we could not study any more. Doing our best to keep ourselves and comrades accountable to the end goal of being able to assist someone in keeping their oral hygiene in its best state. There are many who can attest to how not having good oral hygiene effects their self-esteem. If we had not made and continue to make the sacrifice of giving up family time, hangout time, and sleep time, there is a human being out there that will suffer because we did not do our part.

Sacrifices Are Necessary to Pass the Test

The sacrifices made to excel and achieve our goals are essential. From January to May 1990, I can say I had not realized what the significance of sacrifice is. Because I had not experienced the power of God in a way where there are visible changes in my human behavior that demonstrate I passed this test. BUT (Believers Understanding Truth) while making a physical sacrifice with my mind and body I learned there are great outcomes when you surrender. Everyone who passed the test written and hands on graduated to the phase of having actual patients to provide care to.

Yes, after the sixteen weeks I achieved the educational goal of becoming a dental hygienist, now comes the next test. Am I able to truly help each individual patient who sits in my chair? Am I equipped to serve them with the skills and knowledge I received during my training? Now, I know I used an actual event of achieving higher skill levels for a profession. But little did I know then, being a dental hygienist tied right into who I am. As a result, I was able to not just provide care for their oral cavity in a lot of cases I was able to provide care for their spiritual being as well. As they sat in the chair in a laid-back semi resting position. Many times, I was able to notice there was something stopping individuals from moving forward with an overall better quality of life. The first order of business when the moments of intuition would come up was to get their heart healed.

The sacrifice of leaving my comfortable home and gaining insight into oral health and having a few years of intense God instruction, opened opportunities for me to speak life to individuals who I would not have run into or had a chance to fully engage them on the street. I was coming into this recognition that I was born to help others get through the process along their journey. Suppose for a moment that I would not have followed the instructions of my teachers, or I did not pass my test; it is probable that I may have caused physical damage to my patients. If I were not properly trained and now skilled.

I must admit, there were times when there was physical pain, but that came when the individual I was treating had allowed plaque to build where it was causing damage and the only way to get rid of it is to remove the thing, in this case plaque, which is the real reason for the pain. Once this is removed the persons gum tissue can begin to heal and most times when their oral health is intact, they tend to feel better about themselves. They smile more and the act of smiling is healing. BUT, if, I had not sacrificed this may not have taken place. I remember vividly how the dentist in the operatory next to mine would come over and ask if I would pray with his patient because of circumstances in their lives.

Following Your Inner Instructions

It is imperative that we know how to follow instructions. I was just reading in Proverbs 1 how we are to be fully acquainted with wisdom and instructions because this is how we get understanding. Despising instructions produces a fool, which this writer describes as someone who experiments without thought. Having no idea which way to go or what to do. Without comprehending the insight from the instructions for wise living foolish tactics may be employed and keep you from living a life of abundance as God intended.

Take moments of becoming completely, totally, and absolutely submerged in wisdom and instructions as a great gift to help in the process of recognizing, the distinguished, unique person you are. Every test of life requires the best of who we are to always show up as. I have this saying to Always "BE" Awesome! No not perfect or without emotion, simply the best image of you is always there. It's the choice we make that determines who shows up. Imagine, the brutality of condensing a two-year college level curriculum into four months. This arduous training and testing produced one of the best dental hygienists, if I do say so myself. The test that seemed insurmountable turned out it was not impossible to climb because I had immersed myself in the process of studying, I was able to show myself approved and was not faced with being ashamed because I was willing to make the momentary sacrifice. That quick span of time having days and nights of pressure could not match up to healing physically and spiritually. I am a vessel used to give copious love and grace to help others as they move forward and push through their own personal test. Those sixteen weeks of test and trials of being pregnant, away from home, my daughter was a test of my will and how willing I was to endure for the sole purpose of helping someone else. It instilled in me that because you passed that test you are strong enough to pass the next one.

Psalm 32:8 Living Bible

8 I will instruct you (says the Lord) and guide you along the best pathway for your life; I will advise you and watch your progress.

We are all distinguished by the test. The test proves you are focused on purpose and will do what it takes to follow Gods path for your life.

Once I passed all the test at the end of the sixteen weeks my records reflected that I was as a dental hygienist. What have some of your tests proven you to be? What great exploits have you done? What are your distinguishing qualities?

Exodus 16:4 Living Bible

4 Then the Lord said to Moses, "Look, I'm going to rain down food from heaven for them. Everyone can go out each day and gather as much food as he needs. And I will test them in this, to see whether they will follow my instructions or not.

Every day, we receive what I call the gift of 24; since there are 24 hours in one day, I call it a gift. The gift is from God. Here are even more reasons to get excited about the gift. Each day the children of Israel were fed, they did not even have to go look for it. When it arrived all they had to do was gather it and get as much as they needed. That is a key word, needed. Here is the part most of us miss. The test. What is the test? The test, come on lean in, is to not take more than you need. We cannot allow human wants to creep in. Those things we believe satisfy our human perceptions.

According to study.com, "a need is something that is needed to survive. A want is something that an individual desires but would be able to live without." Confusion sets in because the things we desire have the predisposition to turn into us believing these are things we cannot live without. Let some individuals lose their cell phone and you may see a very different human standing in front of you. Go ahead laugh, you know it is true. This notion of there are things we cannot live without can take us so far off course it becomes difficult to find our way back. If you are having difficulty finding your way back to your true authenticity, take this moment to ask for instructions and everything needed to make that happen will arise inside of you. Do not worry about if it does not feel or look like you think it should be. Just trust in faith and faith will produce evidence you are heading in the right direction. Abandon old desires and believe everything you need to sustain your life is raining down.

Liberation

Do not stifle your own freedom by trying to revive things that are dead, they no longer exist. There are things in life that no longer cause you to be your authentic self. These things can cause a sudden death to the real you. This is where we need to have what I call discernment. Insight or discernment is a necessary to have to know who you are. A continual pursuit of having this awareness makes us the expert of who we are and what we are to be. We must become proficient in being us. No more hiding behind our past. Speak it, I am breaking free to BE ____! Now you fill in the blank(s). You make the difference you are the main influence of all the positive effects that occur in your life. When our heart, mind, and soul are positioned correctly the reality is we are capable of occupying space. Having our heart, mind, and soul in a state of awareness about who we are is the only way to ensure we are on point in life. Holding on to the past person who was not believing in you placed a veil over the eyes of our heart and made us believe a myriad of things about ourselves. Most of the thoughts were not ones that would make us feel deserving of the greatness we possess. I want us to walk in total freedom today. Liberation from all things that hide the authentic you.

Walking in freedom just simply means we no longer allow our thoughts to enslave us to things that move us away from the genuine you. I remember when I was in my mid-twenties, I wanted to wear clothes that at the time most thought they did not match. Well, here we are some thirty years later, and it is acceptable. Just think if I had followed the passion of who I really am and allowed the artist in me to BE. Guess what, those days are over that veil is removed and my understanding to who I am is clear. Today and every day from this moment I pray you are clearing your path to follow your passions. No more mask on our BEING. No more covering the real you. At this time, the world is experiencing a pandemic and mask are required in places. I am writing this as the Centers for Disease Control and Prevention would as they are telling us what is needed for protection. Today, a greater agency is giving instructions, the Center for Dismantling Constraints declare the mask mandate over your life to be permanently taken away. It is time your intrinsic nature and indispensable qualities are consciously free.

BE free to live in the vibrancy of your colorful soul dancing to the rhythm of your heartbeat.

My freedom and yours, is not predicated upon what another person thinks or feels. We are not obligated to put a mask on what makes me free. I am thinking about when I lived in Egypt and an Egyptian shop owner invited me to dinner during Ramadan. Now why would they ask this woman who proclaims another life guide to attend their dinner during this sacred time? It was obvious this freedom we all participated in although from different viewpoints did not affect our human relationship and we were able to glean from one another. While I ate, I did not ask them what is this or what is that? It was an honor for human beings from another country, another dialect, many different facets of philosophy, to give me an invitation. Because they invited me, I accepted, and it did not make me any less of a who I am or what I believe. What I am saying is never turn down an opportunity to demonstrate your freedom because in your freedom we display love, and we are operating from a pure place. We must keep our freedom convictions solid. Stay you. Stay free. Demonstrating your freedom among those who may not have reached where you are is beneficial and wonderful to be able to do. Our life can display a story of how love compels liberty, and it does not promote an oppressed mind.

Humph! Okay, that is a thing an oppressed mind. It is of this writer's opinion an oppressed mind is one that continues to over please, especially trying to please something that will not provide the needed ingredients to accomplish your life's process of self-actualization. In other words, it does not serve you. According to Ayesh Perera, self-actualization "is the complete realization of one's potential, and the full development of one's abilities and appreciation for life." I welcome this definition; having a mind that is dominated and exploited by fear of discovery will not perceive or become aware of who they are. To come to full development, a key component is being able to realize. In my second book, there is a part which speaks of not even being able to realize that you are numb and not engaged in life. When the mind is oppressed, it loses its ability to understand and having no understanding renders you completely paralyzed to fulfilling purpose.

Again, stay free, stay you. Someone is waiting for you to recognize your potential and begin to put in the work required to fully develop your aptness. Your magic in the earth. You notice when someone is very good at something those who witness you are in awe. That is your power of realization. Think about Lebron

James, he began developing his talent and through realization was able to demonstrate many instants of greatness, with his magic on the court. The magic on the court gave him provision to spread the magic to those who may not have that same magic, they may be great engineers, doctors, scientists, but that is their magic, and we must own our own magic. Lebron did. The place where we flow freely. Almost like typing these words on these pages at many points it is free flowing of a power within creating magic that bounces off the pages or screens and ignites the fire of passion in you. Now you want to pull out your magic and show it off to the world. Come on let us see how it works. Freely flowing in your purpose that gives others hope to move forward giving them hope to realize. Hope to recognize the person in you is not so strange. Remember there will always be someone or something that will try and see how free you are and want to test you. Do not cave, remain strong never allowing you or anyone else put a restraint on your mind. Trying to set limitations on your greatness and on you believing that you are great. You are free from the confines of your mind when it wants to say you are limited. You are a boundless creative being who once you realize it will fall deeply in love with you.

The Wrong Impression of Love

During my 18-year military career I worked in the dental field. There were several departments who utilized what we call impression material, and it was used for many procedures. Let me name a few you may have experienced this yourself. These impressions may be used in creating mouth guards, retainers, accurate models, whitening trays, crowns, veneers, bridges, dentures, just to name a few.

Dental impressions are an imprint of the teeth and the mouth.

You may be wondering what this has to do with me or anyone else for that matter and how we made or make decisions concerning love. Stick with me here, I promise you we will get to the meat of the matter, but it takes time to peel back the layers. It took time to get here to this point of you reading and receiving ideas and me releasing my ideas on to these pages for the purpose of getting us to have the right impression of love.

Back to the dental impressions. When an imprint is taken the assistant must ensure it is done with accuracy. This individual must provide instructions to the patient well enough for them gain an understanding of the severity of getting this right. If for some reason the impression is off even by a millimeter this will cause more work for the dentist, more time for the patient because you will have to return to the dental office several times, take off work, possibly lose money, and God forbid whatever the impression was created for does not fit properly. This is more duplicate use of the dentist time. In this industry time is money no one wants to work on the same apparatus multiple times.

Okay, let's explore this from the standpoint of humanity and how we form impressions or thoughts and ideas of love. Think of the assistant who walks toward you with this tray like device aiming to place it in your mouth. Back in my military days the trays were cold steal. They are coming to put something foreign in the place where you allow sound to come through and substance to enter your body. If they have no clue how to use this instrument it can cause gag reflexes to become agitated and being in this profession for the length of time I was, there were a few occasions a reflex was stimulated easily if the person had just eaten. If you get my drift; that made for a not so pleasant experience.

Now, think of this not so pleasant experience happening when the person or persons who are responsible for knowing how to maneuver through this process called life are living through distorted ideas. Like the assistant who is trusted to understand this process, but there are times when you are their first patient, and they were misled when they were being trained. They are forming new ideas on how to use the device and you are the guinea pig.

This is how we as humans can go about life. It is through our lack of experiences along the journey that provide the misdirection. Make sure you are staying true to your process and not cutting corners. It is okay to go through a rough patch in life we just cannot afford to stay stuck in the patch. I remember sometime the impression tray would even get stuck in the patient's mouth. Well, it appeared to be stuck, BUT (Believers Understanding Truth) understand when I remove this I still need to make sure it stays intact to produce a great product. Something that is going to enhance this patient's ability to maintain or have an oral cavity that will last them a lifetime. Remember, there is always a through. We must follow the process. It may not be as appealing as we think it should be. Making sure we mix the ingredients of life right, so our minds do not become warped with the intentions of others. I know firsthand the journey will bring moments of warped ideas and thoughts from outside sources and the impression then becomes faulty.

Stay in Alignment

We cannot allow our impression of who we are to be wrapped in outside entities opinions of you. Their vision is impaired because they can only see it through their eyes. Now the purpose you were created for is out of alignment and you are not able to be used for your intended purpose. When the dental impression is out of alignment this will cause the patient's ability to chew properly to be off center. Because of a defect the use of this vital source of digestion to receive adequate nutrition to live and be healthy is altered.

This gives us a view of important it is we remain aligned with our life purpose. Having the necessary ingredients for living a healthy life that has substance and meaning goes hand in hand with our impressions of who we are, and how we are to love ourselves to life. If we allow anything other than love to produce what is in our heart and mind, most likely our experiences have been shaped with the wrong impression. To top it off most likely the level of value we have for ourselves is probably much smaller. It is significant to say here, the trays come in different sizes, representing the value we put on our purpose. Make sure you use the right size tray to capture the complete impression of who you are. This way you are not left struggling to gain a clear viewpoint on how to demonstrate love to yourselves and others. Show yourself every day, when it is raining, or sunshine blue sky's make it your point to love you. Number one priority is what you believe is in you.

Look at this in your minds view, there are those of us who have experienced inaccurate ideas or have not felt true forms of love neither have we been able to see it demonstrated in human form. Therefore, leaving our impression of love is skewed. It is distorted making its formative process lack the ability to build true value. When we do not learn the value of love, we do not learn the value of who we are, this can take us down a path of that famous saying "looking for love in all the wrong places." Why because we have the wrong idea or impression of what it is and where it is. Love is a verb, and you will know it when you see it, feel it, and embrace it.

Love in Action

When love is received properly as it is given in its pure state, it causes a rise in action and our life begins to take on new form. There is an exhibition of beauty that can be felt a life-giving force making imprints of patience, kindness, generosity, humility, discipline, freedom to BE real and, have a knowing that you can BE truthful with yourself.

We begin to think differently about life, who we are, and how we will produce these unction's and declarations of greatness we have found. We are ignited to start looking within to unlock the chains that have held our mind's view of who we are for far too long.

The criteria needed to unlock the unconditional love that changes our wrong impression to a pure impression of love is starting with you giving yourself permission to offer these things to you first.

- Patience – the capacity to agree to being you.
- Kindness – become your own friend. Be nice to you.
- Generosity – Allow yourself the freedom to be you.
- Humility – Walk in quiet strength and confidence. Trust you.
- Discipline – There is a consistent action needed to be you.

Colossians 3:12 The Message Translation

So, chosen by God for this new life of love, dress in the wardrobe God picked out for you: compassion, kindness, humility, quiet strength, discipline.

Use the above list as a litmus test determining how effective we are in demonstrating our impression of loving ourselves to life. To a life of productivity and prosperity. Today allow your thoughts of love to be formed using this guaranteed method to follow while living this new life of loving you. Keep this as a rule, if what you experience does not meet the characteristics, understand that you cannot and will not go backwards. You have set healthy boundaries and now you have requirements to accepting what respects your value. On this journey do not allow yourself to come down too heavy on you either. Just follow your heart always having the purest of intensions. We can do this now because our heart is working again. This will lead you to a love impression that is aligned with the true authentic you. Every day I wake up I affirm my position with these words.

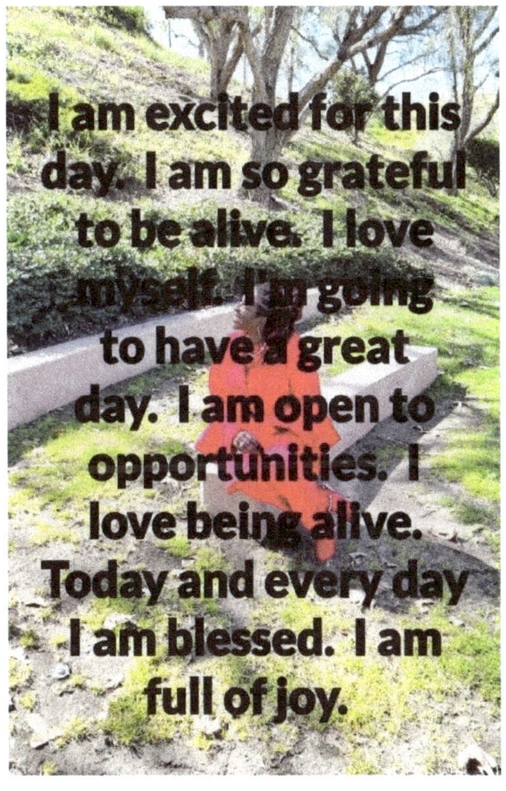

Do Not Let Pain Win

This chapter title has been my life's moto for the past 25 years. I was in a life changing accident in 1997, while serving in the United States Army. That was a physical injury which to this day I still have pain. However, that is not the topic of this chapter. Here is where we deal with emotional pain from the ills that life has and will throw our way. For instance, yesterday I came to the realization that I needed to let something go and it caused me internal pain. There was heartache. At that moment I also had to recognize and appreciate that I was doing what was best for me. There are times when we do not realize, recognize, and certainly have no appreciation for who we are, and we let physical and emotional pain win. Today, that will no longer be our story. Today all pain whether it is in the body or in the mind will be used as a catalyst. Yes, memories of moments which hurt sneak into my thoughts because I guarantee you, I do not consciously conjure them up.

It is a sneak attack, and every day we are discovering that the power within us is more powerful than any attack. Sneak or upfront. Now we have a weapon to use when the memories find it necessary to pop up, we find it necessary to use it for our good. Because we have been doing the work to prepare for life. When situations come up, as they will on a continual basis, but everything is not necessarily bad that shows up as stress. I am writing this book during prom season. This is a very exciting time for graduates and their families. However, it is also a time of finality to something which was a constant in a person's life. Now at this major turning point the question comes up, what is next? Here is where we need the preparation to pay off. Providing us with solid tools for working out life circumstances.

As I was studying to write this chapter, I found this nugget that gave me a burst of excitement and overstanding. I hope your experience will be similar or better. The word tool, according to Microsoft search comes "from a Germanic base meaning prepare." I teach this class called "Tools for Everyday Living," because we need an arsenal of drive that will equip us to produce what we need daily. The ability to use life as a tool is our best plan. We will use life by making it our catalyst. It's the spark you will need to change any negative into fuel to motivate, inspire, and transform your life.

Catalyst will guide us in determining what is next and be the cause of becoming aware of who we are, acknowledging our value and understanding our worth causes us to continue. In this process of life and following your journey, grasping hold to, and being tenacious about the value we carry in these mortal temples gives you the ability to outlast and conquer anything that comes your way.

You have the power to win. Yes, it will take effort and energy. Your willingness to provoke and invoke your God given strengths of wisdom, knowledge, and understanding should never be compromised. Use your catalyst of wisdom, your clear insight to who you are, to love and be proud of you. If you should need to adjust for the purpose of aligning yourself to be effective on the journey, do that. It is not too late be proud of you realizing, recognizing, and appreciating you gives a huge boost to your esteem. You are the main ingredient in this perpetual process of spiritual amplification. Here is a good message for us all.

Proverbs 4:7 Living Bible

7 Getting wisdom is the most important thing you can do! And with your wisdom, develop common sense and good judgment.

Proverbs 4:7 Amplified Bible

7 "The beginning of wisdom is: Get [skillful and godly] wisdom [it is preeminent]! And with all your acquiring, get understanding [actively seek spiritual discernment, mature comprehension, and logical interpretation].

C **C**almness and clarity in calamity a winning formula for you.

A **A**dventurous in spirit. Demonstrate your freedom.

T **T**enacious grip for understanding and trusting you. Never give up.

A **A**stute in every situation. Tell it oh yeah, I know what you look like.

L **L**oving on you always because there is no other way to do it.

Y **Y**earning for God and more insight always to keep light on our path.

S **S**afety is us diligently protecting and guarding our hearts.

T **T**ake the initiative. No one is going to do it for us!

In life we all have experiences that are unpleasant and unpredictable, but it is solely up to us how we push through and what tools we use to help. I encourage you to apply this one whenever needed. When the memories of some horrific events show up, I show up with my catalyst of peace, bravery, persistence, intelligence, truth, desire to be more, assurance of who I am and seize every opportunity God brings my way. Every moment has a purpose we must be open to the lesson which will produce growth and an unconditional love of self.

To accomplish this, you will need the following:

- Affirmation which gives you emotional support or encouragement.
- The ability to realize -become fully aware of (something) as a fact.
- Recognize you, acknowledge your existence and know that you are valuable.
- Appreciate and recognize your full worth.
- Use your new catalyst as the agent that provokes significant change in your actions.

Each day we are blessed with the gift of 24 (a new day) promise to be your own encouragement, promise to seek to have a keen awareness of what makes you unique, accept and validate your greatness, appreciate all of you, and most importantly when life attempts to dim your light combine all the ingredients and BE your own change agent in that moment. Yes, it is simply just that a moment and you get to choose how you define it. Moments do not identify who we are. We determine how this very brief space in time will be depicted in the theatre of our minds. Because we are whole. Meaning we are at peace with God who is the giver of peace, and this peace ensures there is nothing missing, nothing broken, and nothing out of place "everything is as it should be."

No Longer Fractured

Fractures are tricky. There are cases when an individual may not even be aware of it, as it may start as a hair line fracture. This is a tiny separation caused by continual stress over time. Sounds like that can also be equated to life's pressures; when we are not sure how to deal with them. Therefore, we do not address them and the repeated stress of it will cause deeper damage. I know while you are reading this your mind may automatically divert to pain in our physical body but let me direct us to the emotional pain in the mind. Emotional pain causes fractures in your soul. Imagine there is something, a force tugging at you saying you have purpose. Then out of nowhere you get sucker punched by divorce, death of a loved one, loss of your job and so on. You may have experienced all or one of these circumstances or none, but I guarantee your life brought you something that packed a punch. The next view you see of your purpose has a tear, a breach, a contravention, of the essential part of who you are. Especially, those entrepreneurs who closed a business. There is a huge split right in the middle of your vision. You hear the ripping of your soul. You felt it tear any semblance of hope. I feel it as I put it in writing. Too often we allow disappointments, fears, rejection and whatever else comes along dragging distress, that piles up, gets to heavy and it breaks our human will.

But today, we are stronger and declare we are no longer broken. Hairline fracture, thin and not so noticeable, you know, just a small amount of pain. Note to self here, remember to address all pain no matter how little, big, or enormous. You can and will heal, but do not get fooled into thinking it is not that bad and it grows into something harder to handle. Deal with it immediately.

Then there is the compound fracture that is visible, and others can physically see your wound, you know when there are witnesses who stand around and look, but no one is helping you, or a dislocated fracture, the bone is completely dislodged, and the affected limb does not function effectively. If your leg were disconnected at the kneecap your ability to walk straight would be hampered and it would deter you from walking at all. This reminds me of my time in at what I know now was the end of my military career. I walked approximately 15 feet, and I began to experience excruciating pain my lower back, next thing I know I was on the floor, and many were watching as this happened because I was walking through a large dental office I had been placed in charge of. I was the Non-commissioned Officer in Charge and there I was sitting in the middle of the floor. Not only was my physical ability to walk prevented, but my intestinal fortitude was hampered too. My strength to stand physically and mentally was being challenged. I had many feelings of being disconnected to any productive source at that time. I was in pain and sitting on the floor (the lowest part of the building) with no clue as to what would happen next. That disconnection and what I felt as a tearing away eventually became a strength. Because I spent 18-years of my life serving in the uniform and at that moment having to face the fact that I would no longer be able to wear it as soldier was heartbreaking. I used, not just that heartbreak, but all of them brought me here pouring out my soul on the lines of these pages. With the intent of guiding others who may find themselves sitting at the lowest part of life and desperately want to get up and move in purpose, I hope that I have shared something to lift you up and strengthen your will. Allow these words to invoke courage to believe in you.

Because we overstand, meaning we are enlightened in our knowledge and trust the power we own. We are no longer separated, confused, or disengaged from our journey. We stand having gone through a healing process, made the choice to go about conducting our lives productively, taking solid steps with solid preparation leading us to greatness.

Never again allow your ability to flow to become obstructed, skewed, or broken again to a point of no return. Life is going to bring its stuff. I encourage you to continue building on this strength and know your way is concrete. Know your way is established, confirmed, and unchangeable.

1 Peter 5:10, Amplified Bible

10 After you have suffered for a little while, the God of all grace [who imparts His blessing and favor], who called you to His own eternal glory in Christ, will Himself complete, confirm, strengthen, and establish you [making you what you ought to be].

Say this out loud everyday: Today, I accept that I am no longer fractured, no longer separated from the source of power, no longer disconnected, and broken. I declare my life no longer is filled with cracks of hopelessness, misery, or even thoughts of gloom. Although, some days may appear to have grey clouds, I allow the abundance of light within me to shine on my path and I vow to continue this journey. I walk in confidence, trust, and strength in who I AM. The cracks of my past no longer cast a shadow of darkness over me. Every force that tried to break my spirit and tear me apart is now infused with the power of love.

Moments in the Darkroom

When times are dark, and life doesn't seem to care,
And love is in a distant stare,
Believe it or not,
These are moments that build
Grand Assurance.
Moments of lifting 45-pound spiritual dumbbells
And just like the athlete who will have to
Enter the game for the first time after a horrific injury,
The questions of the past come flooding to the forefront of your thoughts:
Will you be able to do it again?
Will I last? Will I get hurt again?
Abort all the questions of your past. Leave doubt behind.
Because, baby, please understand you are a diamond not glass.

Life will not destroy your destiny. Keep flowing on the journey.
Keep showing up. Keep BEING your best self.
Darkness and despair do not have the ability to stop your shine.
Your glow of possibilities, your light so bright it penetrates the darkest of days.
Singing "this little light of mine I'm gonna let it shine."
Your light so bright it ignites the human soul.
So, when times are dark, don't worry the brilliance of the radiant love from within will beam through the fractured parts and get filled with the healing balm of Gilead.
The salve needed to heal the essence of your soul.
Your soul that produces an anomaly, an abundance of this life-giving force.
An energy that causes others to see the truth of who they are.
(LOL, add in) After that, it's up to them to face your truth or not. I pray you choose to see.

See the light that still radiates through me
The light of wealth shines around me causes the darkness to cease. It causes the darkness to produce the beautiful image of greatness

imprinted on your soul to come alive in full view for the world to see.

Without the power of your light shining through darkness the mystery of you would be hidden. Always remember the darkness has showed you how much power you have and the enormous capacity you possess to carry out your greatness. So, when this portion of time seems sunless overstand out of that space is coming an agent of change. You are the change agent of your soul. Never again will a temporary moment swallow up your dreams and visions, but these dark moments are now destroyed in our enlightenment of the power of love the "The Life-Light blazed out of the darkness; the darkness couldn't put it out." No one can stop your shine. It gives life to all who meet you.

John 1:3-5 Message Bible translation

Everything was created through him;
nothing—not one thing!—
came into being without him.
What came into existence was Life,
and the Life was Light to live by.
The Life-Light blazed out of the darkness;
the darkness couldn't put it out.

www.ingramcontent.com/pod-product-compliance
Lightning Source LLC
LaVergne TN
LVHW050425160826
845677LV00002BA/536

* 9 7 9 8 8 4 7 6 1 1 6 6 4 *